The White House Murder Case
&
Dick and Jane

Director Alan Arkin during rehearsal

Jules
Feiffer

THE
WHITE HOUSE
MURDER CASE
a play in two acts

&

DICK AND JANE
a one-act play

Grove Press, Inc., New York

To Elizabeth Ames
Polly Hanson
and Yaddo

and to
Alan Arkin

President, Parson, Sweeney

The White House
Murder Case

Postmaster General Stiles, Professor Sweeney,
Mrs. Hale

Parson, President, Cole, Sweeney, Stiles

Lieutenant Cutler, General Pratt, Colonel Dawn

The White House Murder Case was first performed at Circle in the Square, New York, on February 18, 1970. Directed by Alan Arkin; produced by Theodore Mann, Paul Libin, Harold Leventhal, and Orin Lehman; sets by Marsha Louis Eck; costumes by Albert Wolsky; lighting by David F. Segal; and with the following cast:

COLONEL DAWN	Dick Libertini
LIEUTENANT CUTLER	Edward J. Moore
GENERAL PRATT	J. J. Barry
PROFESSOR SWEENEY	Anthony Holland
MRS. HALE	Cynthia Harris
POSTMASTER GENERAL STILES	Paul Benedict
ATTORNEY GENERAL COLE	Paul Dooley
SECRETARY OF DEFENSE PARSON	Andrew Duncan
PRESIDENT HALE	Peter Bonerz
CAPTAIN WEEMS	Bob Balaban

Photos from the production:
Sy Friedman—Zodiac Photography

act one

scene one

The time of the play is several presidential elections hence.

The stage is bare, dimly and coldly lit. The sound of bombardment, near and distant. Sudden flashes of light in sync with bombardment. LIEUTENANT CUT-LER and an aide charge across stage. A burst of machine-gun fire and the aide staggers and falls. LIEUTENANT CUTLER drops, and cautiously inches forward. COLONEL DAWN enters, crawling on his belly, and catches up to CUTLER.

DAWN: What's it look like, Lieutenant?

CUTLER: Chico's holed up in there pretty good, sir.

DAWN: You use your 135s on 'im?

CUTLER: Colonel Dawn, we've hit 'im with 290s, 628s, 135s, you name it.

5

DAWN: What seems to be the problem?

CUTLER: Chico's got good ordnance, sir. Damn good ordnance and high morale factor.

DAWN: I want to see this area secured, Lieutenant Cutler.

CUTLER: Sir, we've hit 'im with twelve air strikes: napalm, defoliants, antipersonnels, fragmentation, seminukes. But hardware don't impress Chico. These are fanatics, sir. Lives don't count.

DAWN: General Pratt's scheduled an appearance in this area. I need a good show for General Pratt.

CUTLER: My boys are damn good boys, Colonel Dawn, but Chico is hardnosed.

DAWN: There's no question we'll have to pull back.

CUTLER: I don't anticipate that, sir. But Chico is hardnosed.

DAWN: General Pratt returns to Washington tomorrow. I don't have to stress the importance his report to the President will have on our effort down here. Our effort down here in Brazil is not a popular effort.

CUTLER: No, sir. If we could only use our CB97s.

DAWN: I was not informed CB97s were deployed.

CUTLER: Yes, sir. Deployed but inoperative.

DAWN: I don't have that information.

CUTLER: Yes, sir. If we could make our CB97s operative—

DAWN: Out of the question. Low reliability factor.

CUTLER: Excuse me, sir, but with Chico holed up where he is, my educated guess would rate the reliability factor upwards of eighty percent.

DAWN: It's in violation of the Geneva Convention—

CUTLER: I'm not a politician, sir. But if we want Chico for General Pratt, CB97 is all I know will do the job.

DAWN: You say it's deployed?

CUTLER: Yes, sir.

DAWN: It must have been deployed for a reason. (*Uneasy pause.*) It can't be activated without a KCR.

CUTLER: You have KCR authorization.

DAWN: But if I issued a KCR, it would be based on your recommendation.

CUTLER: Mine is an unofficial recommendation, sir. I don't have authority.

DAWN: I need an official recommendation before I'm authorized to authorize. Now, should I or shouldn't I?

Burst of machine-gun fire. Both crawl backward. GENERAL PRATT *strides in, stares down at them.*

PRATT: What are American troops doing on their knees in front of a bunch of goddamned Brazilians?

CUTLER (*leaps to his feet and salutes*): Tain-hut!

A bullet cuts him down. PRATT *drops.* DAWN *rolls* CUTLER *over.*

DAWN: He's bleeding badly, General Pratt.

PRATT: What's he mumbling?

CUTLER: C—B—9—7—

PRATT: C—B—what?

DAWN: Lieutenant Cutler recommends KCR authorization to activate our CB97s.

PRATT: Does that recommendation meet with your approval, Colonel?

DAWN: I don't have the total picture that you do, General Pratt.

CUTLER: C—B—9—7—

PRATT: It's going to be all right, son. (*To* DAWN.) I'm afraid he's going to have to lose that leg. This may be his last request, Colonel.

DAWN: Then you say go ahead?

PRATT: If you say so.

DAWN: I say so if you say so.

PRATT: He said so?

DAWN: Yes, sir.

PRATT: Well, if he says so and you say so, I'll go along.

DAWN: Am I to interpret that as a go-ahead on KCR authorization, sir?

PRATT: If you say so.

CUTLER: C—B—9—7!

PRATT: Easy, lad. You'll get all the CB97s you want!

CUTLER: God bless you, sir!

DAWN *exits running.*

PRATT: Wait a minute, Colonel Dawn! (*Starts after him.*) Colonel Dawn, come back! (*Stops and removes a red code book from his jacket pocket.*) A–A–A–B–B–B–C–C–CB–CB3–CB7 –CB9–CB91–CB95–CB97! (*Reads.*) Nerve gas! (*To* CUTLER.) I'll break you for this! (*Leaps to his feet and rushes after* DAWN.) Rescind! Rescind! *I rescind!*

Lights fade on battlefield.

Attorney General Cole   *Secretary of Defense Parson*

act one

scene two

Lights up in President Hale's office. Five conference chairs gathered around his desk. Through the window, a view of the Capitol. Behind the President's desk, a door. MRS. HALE *is rapidly leafing through papers on President's desk, as* PROFESSOR SWEENEY *enters from stage right.*

SWEENEY: Mrs. Hale! Those are classified documents!

MRS. HALE: Sweeney, what happened in Brazil? My husband won't tell me a thing!

SWEENEY: You know you're in violation of security, you shouldn't be in here!

MRS. HALE: My husband's office? Don't be an ass.

SWEENEY: The President's office!

MRS. HALE: Emmy's been president of two foundations and a university, and he's never kept me out of his office. I'd like to see him try! Now, what's this all about, Sweeney? You know I'll find out anyhow.

SWEENEY: Do you enjoy seeing me in trouble with the President?

MRS. HALE: Very much. I've noticed a humane streak in you, Sweeney. It only surfaces when you violate your conscience. It's the one thing in you I've found to admire.

SWEENEY: Oh, Evelyn—(*He tries to embrace her. She eludes him.*) Is there no way I can make you take me seriously?

MRS. HALE: Nothing personal, Sweeney. I can't take anyone seriously who works for the government.

SWEENEY: This streak of anarchism in you, Evelyn —it sometimes so infuriates me I want to shake you.

MRS. HALE: Drop a bomb on me instead. Isn't that the traditional relief for frustration around here?

SWEENEY: How can I make you believe the number of bombs I keep from being dropped each day?

MRS. HALE: Of what possible threat is Brazil to the United States?

SWEENEY: That's a policy question. I'm in research and development.

MRS. HALE: Is that why we're in Brazil? New wars in order to test your new research?

SWEENEY: I'm as much committed to peace as you

are! And I get a lot more done than those paci-
fist–draft dodger–demonstrator–jailbirds your
heart so bleeds over! I work from the inside!

MRS. HALE: Ah! And which inside work of yours
brought forth this extraordinary meeting at eight
o'clock on a Sunday morning? That's what I
want to find out! Tell me, Sweeney! (SWEENEY
begins to unravel. She advances on him.) For
me, Sweeney.

STILES (*enters from stage right, freezes*): Madam
First Lady, Professor Sweeney. (*A broad grin.*)
A good, good morning.

MRS. HALE *coldly exits past* STILES. *He grins
nastily as she passes.* COLE *enters from stage
right, looking after* MRS. HALE *as she departs.*

COLE: That woman—

STILES (*to* SWEENEY): What was she doing in here?

SWEENEY: Your guess is as good as mine. Good
morning, Tim.

STILES (*suspicious*): Morning.

SWEENEY: Newton?

COLE: Professor Sweeney. (*To* STILES.) You heaɪ
about her with the sit-ins at the Justice Department last week?

SWEENEY (*incredulous*): No!

STILES (*grinning*): Yeah?

COLE: Right outside my office. Told 'em their cause
was right and they should keep on fighting. Had

to threaten the entire press corps with conspiracy indictments to kill the story. The file I have on that woman.

STILES: Those damn files. Is there a politician in this country you couldn't break, Newt?

COLE: I'd like to prosecute you for your lousy mail service.

STILES: The Postmaster General's job is to deliver the vote. The mail's incidental. Which is what worries me about Sweeney's mess in Brazil—

SWEENEY (*outraged*): *My* mess?

STILES: Six weeks before the presidential election is not the time to test out poison gas.

SWEENEY: That's top secret information!

STILES: I'm national chairman of the party, Professor. You can't keep your little experiments from me. Next time you gas American troops, do it after the first Tuesday in November.

SWEENEY: This discussion is in violation of national security!

STILES: The gooks know about the gas, the Postmaster General isn't supposed to. That's America for you.

COLE: Chico's, Tim. Not gooks.

STILES: Chico's. I lose track of the wars, they come so fast.

SWEENEY: Gooks! Chico's! Don't you see how you dehumanize by using those terms?

STILES: Sweeney's hanging around the First Lady too much.

COLE: I wish the President would muzzle that woman.

STILES: We're lucky she doesn't talk him into muzzling us. (*He laughs.*)

COLE (*angry*): It's not a joke! It dumfounds me how he can face up to the Russians and the Chinese and the Arabs and the Africans and the Brazilians—but won't face up to his own wife.

PARSON (*enters from stage right*): Ah, my favorite subject, I see. Morning, men.

STILES: Biff.

COLE: 'Lo, Biff.

SWEENEY (*half-mocking*): Mr. Secretary of Defense.

PARSON: The man of the hour. What happened to your Peace Gas, Sweeney?

STILES: Is that what he calls it?

COLE: Peace Gas? How many did it kill?

SWEENEY: Reports vary.

PARSON: Seven hundred and fifty troops. All ours.

STILES: Whew!

SWEENEY: This is premature. CB97 does not always result in death.

STILES: What does it result in, if not death?

SWEENEY: We don't know. Much depends on climatic conditions.

PARSON: It paralyzed another ninety. Including the Army Chief of Staff.

STILES: General Pratt! That's news to me.

COLE: Your intelligence isn't up to mine, Tim. I knew it by 9:30 last night.

PARSON: I was only informed at 9:45, and I'm the Secretary of Defense!

STILES: Don't bicker, boys. The Secretary of State still hasn't been told.

> STILES *and* PARSON *laugh.* COLE *grins.* SWEENEY *looks concerned.*

SWEENEY: Why isn't he here?

PARSON: Still in the doghouse, is he?

COLE: He made a damned fool of himself over the Brazilian intervention.

STILES: If he had any horse sense—

SWEENEY: But he opposed the intervention. So did you, Stiles—and you too, Cole.

PARSON: Not after the President made his decision.

SWEENEY: He's the oldest member of the cabinet. Maybe four wars in six years finally got to him.

STILES: If you can't stand the heat, stay out of the kitchen.

PARSON: Who said that? Harry Truman?

STILES: It wasn't Chairman Mao.

PARSON: The questions is—(*Stops himself.*)

COLE: What, Biff?

PARSON: Forget it.

SWEENEY: Can the President stand the heat? Isn't that your question, Mr. Secretary?

PARSON: You're perceptive, Sweeney. I'll say that for you.

COLE: You think the President has doubts about our Brazilian commitment? I can't go along with you on that, Biff.

PARSON: He's never been happy with it.

COLE: Who is?

STILES: Not me.

SWEENEY: Two years, and what do we have to show for it? Twenty-five thousand dead.

PARSON: Those losses are acceptable. A drop in the bucket compared to the African war. We're learning every day.

STILES: It could be a damned expensive education with elections six weeks away.

COLE: And peace conspirators everywhere. I indict a thousand today, a thousand more riot to-morrow.

STILES: Peace riots are water off a duck's back to a man in politics as long as the President.

PARSON: I'm not worried about the riots getting to him. It's that woman getting to him—that's what I lose sleep over. She's worth four divisions of enemy troops.

COLE: I threatened her once with indictment. She laughed.

STILES: You guys take her too seriously. The country's amused by her.

SWEENEY: She's a serious woman!

COLE: She has no right to laugh at me.

PARSON: She doesn't think logically.

COLE: She must be stopped.

PARSON: That woman—

COLE: That woman—

PRESIDENT (*enters from stage right*): Good morning, gentlemen.

All rise.

I'm sorry I'm delayed. (*Smiles.*) Mrs. Hale wanted to have several words with me. Please be seated. Secretary Parson, you are well this morning?

PARSON: Well as can be expected, Mr. President.

PRESIDENT: Mr. Attorney General?

COLE: Good morning, Mr. President.

PRESIDENT: I think I recognized your golf clubs outside my office.

COLE: I was hoping I could talk you into a game after the meeting, sir.

PRESIDENT (*sighs*): Ah, if only. I took a few practice strokes with your driver. I couldn't resist.

COLE: My driver is your driver, Mr. President.

PRESIDENT: You don't play golf do you, Professor Sweeney?

SWEENEY: No, Mr. President.

PRESIDENT: You might take it up. It's a restful game. I won't ask you how you are this morning, Tim. You are always the same.

STILES: Terrible.

PRESIDENT: I sympathize. My spies tell me you toured the mail room earlier this morning. No man should be forced to see such sights before breakfast. I sometimes wish we were able to slow all forms of communication as successfully as we slow the U.S. mails.

STILES: I think you enjoy my misery, Mr. President.

PRESIDENT: Not at all. The Secretary of State will not be joining us this morning. He had some—um— paper work. The Secretary of Defense has brought his charts, I see.

PARSON: Yes, sir.

PRESIDENT: Then let's take a look at them.

PARSON (*mounts charts on easel. With a pointer*): This is Brazil.

Lights fade on President's office.

Captain Weems

act one

scene three

Lights up on battlefield. An eerie green light. CAPTAIN WEEMS *leans over* LIEUTENANT CUTLER, *bandaging his head.*

CUTLER (*groans*): C–B—9—7—

WEEMS: It's easier breathing now. I think the worst is over.

CUTLER: I must have passed out. The CB97—it blew back on us.

WEEMS: I don't know what that is.

CUTLER: Who are you?

WEEMS: Captain Weems, medical corps.

CUTLER: You saved my life.

WEEMS: We're not out of it yet.

CUTLER: Don't tell me—I owe you my life.

WEEMS: We'd better get moving before the gas gets us.

CUTLER: This is gas?

WEEMS: I don't know what it is, but it's not fog and it's all green. What can it be but gas?

CUTLER: Why aren't we choking?

WEEMS: Could it be a different kind of gas?

CUTLER: I don't know anything about it. I always tried to do what I thought was right. I was trying to protect my men. That's primary! **Maybe** you'd better leave me.

WEEMS: We'd better get back.

CUTLER: All I had in mind was the welfare of my men. You're a doctor?

WEEMS: Yes.

CUTLER: You have to think of the welfare of your patients. That's primary, right? Is that or isn't that primary?

WEEMS: I don't want to hang around here a minute longer than we have to.

CUTLER: How old are you, Captain Weems?

WEEMS: Twenty-seven.

CUTLER: I'm twenty-eight. Where are you from?

WEEMS: Cleveland.

CUTLER: I'm from White Plains, New York.

WEEMS: Lieutenant—

CUTLER: You're a doctor, right? Tell me: why doesn't it ever turn out right?

WEEMS: Best to get it off your chest.

CUTLER: What are you writing down?

WEEMS: Notes.

CUTLER: What's your favorite number?

WEEMS: Twenty-seven.

CUTLER: Mine's twenty-eight. What's your favorite color?

WEEMS: White.

CUTLER: Mine's white too. You married?

WEEMS: We'd better get moving.

CUTLER: You married?

WEEMS: Yes.

CUTLER: Any kids?

WEEMS: Two kids. A boy and a girl.

CUTLER: How old?

WEEMS: The boy's five, the girl's three.

CUTLER: Five and three. That makes eight. You're twenty-seven. Twenty-seven and eight make thirty-five. That's okay. Oh, yeah—how old is your wife?

WEEMS: Twenty-one.

CUTLER: That spoils it. It's not advisable to talk to many people. We'd better get moving.

WEEMS: Let's talk.

CUTLER: We'd better get moving. My leg feels much better.

WEEMS: What leg?

CUTLER: My wounded leg.

WEEMS: You mean the leg lying over there?

CUTLER: My leg. (*Feels for it.*) I've lost my leg.

WEEMS: You were groaning. I was trying to find you. I stepped on it. It broke right off.

CUTLER: Serves me right. I don't feel any pain. Do you mind helping me onto my feet—foot, Captain?

WEEMS *helps him up. They stagger a few steps.*

Are you sure you're a doctor?

WEEMS: I bandaged your head, didn't I?

Lights fade on battlefield.

act one

scene four

Lights up on President's office.

PARSON (*at chart*): This is the Mato Grosso where current fighting is in progress. The fighting is centered at five points. (*Indicates.*) In the north, northeast, northwest, southwest, and southeast.

PRESIDENT: In fact, everywhere.

PARSON: These are tough little guys we're fighting, Mr. President.

PRESIDENT: Are we losing the Mato Grosso, Mr. Parson?

PARSON: We're taking heavier losses than projected but, no, sir, we are not losing. The Mato Grosso will be secured, no question. But there are setbacks, and Operation Total Win was one of them. (*Points to new chart.*) The aim of Operation Total Win was to defuse the threat of an enemy buildup in response to our last offensive. This called for air and artillery strikes followed by massive assaults along the entire south-east-west frontier. From points A to K.

PRESIDENT: Under whose command was Operation Total Win?

PARSON: The late Colonel Frank R. Dawn of the 299th. On the seventeenth of September—

PRESIDENT: Two days ago.

PARSON: Yes, sir. At 1600 hours, the combat zone was toured by Army Chief of Staff General Maurice Pratt. During General Pratt's inspection a surprise enemy counterattack necessitated a withdrawal along . . . (*indicates on new map*) . . . points A, B, C, D, E, F, and G to straighten out our lines. An immediate counterattack at 2100 hours was mounted by the 295th, 297th, and 299th, and we regained our positions here, point A, here, point C, here, point E, and here, G but became stalled here, point B, here, point D, and here, point F, where we underwent heavy artillery bombardment from enemy 9s and 10s mounted . . . (*new map*) at here P, here Q, here R, and here S. All subsequent efforts, including twelve air strikes, failed to dislodge the enemy. At 2330 hours a CB97 Nerve Agent was released on enemy positions P, Q, R, and S. The CB97s were artillery-launched from positions A-1, C-1, E-1, and here, G-1. The anticipated results of the Nerve Agent were counterachieved by a sudden shift in wind, as indicated by these wavy lines on the map here. The CB97s are reported to have contaminated the following areas: A-1, C-1, E-1, and, with high probability, G-1. We are at a temporary contact lapse with G-1, and the situation there is still to be confirmed. That summarizes the situation to date.

PRESIDENT: The CB97, in effect, was fired on our own troops.

PARSON: It was fired against the enemy, sir, and would have worked—but for the meteorological variants.

PRESIDENT: How many fatalities?

PARSON: From the CB97?

PRESIDENT (*impatient*): Yes. Yes.

PARSON: Seven hundred and fifty.

PRESIDENT: How many paralyzed?

PARSON: The count is now up to ninety. There may be more. The area is still not decontaminated.

SWEENEY: I would be cautious about those figures, Mr. President. CB97 has certain progressive side effects, the full value of which have yet to be verified.

PRESIDENT: What is the condition of General Pratt?

PARSON: He suffered loss of sight which may or may not be permanent, paralysis of the left side of his body which may or may not be permanent, and permanent damage to the larynx.

PRESIDENT: Is he present for this meeting?

PARSON: He is.

PRESIDENT: Will we be able to communicate with him?

PARSON: Yes, sir. His voice is miked.

PRESIDENT: Ask him in here, please.

> PARSON *exits stage right, re-enters escorting* GENERAL PRATT. PRATT, *in uniform, walks stiffly, wears dark glasses, carries a cane. His face is broken out with sores.*

How are you, General Pratt?

PRATT (*speaks gutturally through throat mike*): Never better, sir.

PRESIDENT: You get around very well.

PRATT: I'm an old night fighter, Mr. President.

PRESIDENT: Allow me to express the hope of all of us in the executive branch for your rapid recovery and return to duty.

PRATT: I'm an old war horse, Mr. President.

PRESIDENT: General Pratt, what light can you bring —uh—what can you tell us about this ghastly affair?

PRATT: Colonel Dawn, the mission command officer for Operation Total Win received in my presence a recommendation from his intelligence officer, Lieutenant Cutler, to initiate the dispersal of the toxic chemical agent CB97. Colonel Dawn concurred in this recommendation and immediately instituted KCR authorization.

PRESIDENT: I was under the assumption that no one under the rank of general had KCR authorization.

PRATT: That is correct, sir. Colonel Dawn had RCK authorization which, in the heat of battle, he understandably confused with KCR authorization. RCK, KCR.

PRESIDENT (*sighs*): You have KCR authorization, do you not, General Pratt?

PRATT: Yes, sir. When I became apprised of the significance of CB97 dispersal, I sought to countermand Colonel Dawn's order. However, I was too late and Colonel Dawn and his staff had fallen by the time I reached Command Headquarters.

PRESIDENT: Why was the gas not lethal to you?

PRATT: I arrived at Command Headquarters seven to ten minutes after dispersal.

SWEENEY: General Pratt?

PRATT: Sir?

SWEENEY: On the basis of evidence in the field, can you draw any conclusions about the span of CB97 effectiveness?

PRATT: My own conclusion is that there is a declining scale of effectiveness after six minutes. For example, the gas operated at close to peak effectiveness on Colonel Dawn and his troops.

But it was no more than fifty percent effective in terms of myself. I was blinded, paralyzed on my left side, suffered second degree facial burns, and received damage to my voice.

SWEENEY: I would rate that higher than fifty percent, General Pratt, in that the side effects you describe are every bit as helpful to us in terms of pacification—

PRATT: I would agree completely.

SWEENEY: I can't tell you how valuable your information is to us. One more question. Is it your opinion that if not for the sudden shift in wind, CB97 would have paid off?

PRATT: No question. With the integration of electronic wind control supports, I would not write off CB97 as an effective weapon in our peace arsenal.

PARSON: Then you do not fault Colonel Dawn for ordering CB97 dispersal?

PRATT: Other than the procedural oversight on authorization, it is my opinion Colonel Dawn made a correct decision at the time he made it. Five minutes later that decision was inappropriate.

PARSON: Then you are completely satisfied.

PRATT: Yes, sir. According to aerial photographs and intelligence estimates, enemy losses are twenty-five times higher than our own.

SWEENEY: I would very much like to see those estimates.

PRATT: They are classified cosmic.

PARSON: I'll arrange to have them released to you.

SWEENEY: Thank you.

PARSON: It'll take a few days.

PRATT: Ten days.

SWEENEY: This can't wait ten days.

PRATT: I'm sorry, Professor Sweeney. Release from cosmic takes ten days.

PRESIDENT: I am sure the research aspects of this catastrophe hold endless fascination, but I am not a scientist. I am the President of the United States six weeks before an election. Can anyone suggest what I say to the American people about the death of seven hundred and fifty American soldiers by an American-made gas?

PARSON: I think you'll find if you prorate these casualties, Mr. President—

PRATT: These are feasible casualties—

PRESIDENT: These are illegal casualties. Mr. Attorney General?

COLE: Yes. The fact of the matter is that all chemical and biological weapons were outlawed by the last Geneva Convent—

SWEENEY (*interrupts*): We didn't sign it—we didn't sign it!

COLE: Nevertheless, we signaled general approv—

SWEENEY: I'm very sorry—we didn't sign it.

PRESIDENT: Is it your view, Professor Sweeney, that these deaths are perfectly legal?

SWEENEY: Good heavens, of course they're legal. It's research and development. Why must we always tie our own hands?

COLE: It may not violate the letter of the law, but it violates the spirit of the law.

PRESIDENT: We mustn't appear casual about the law.

PARSON: *International* law? Aren't we being a little legalistic?

STILES: We don't want to be charged with respect for law at home and contempt for it abroad.

COLE: No, not in these times.

STILES: It could put us in a bad light.

SWEENEY: Only because the public is unaware of the tremendous peace-keeping potential—

STILES: Of nerve gas?!

PRATT: The American people will stand behind their command officers.

PRESIDENT: I couldn't agree more, General Pratt. Once they are informed on the issues.

COLE: And they haven't been informed.

PARSON: This is too complex an issue for public debate.

PRESIDENT: I'm inclined to agree with Secretary Parson. Well, there's certain to be a leak. We will have to leak it first and have ready an explanation. Which may be difficult since the public is under the impression we have discontinued production of poison gas.

PARSON: We *have* discontinued production, sir.

SWEENEY: But not research.

PRESIDENT: Research has continued?

SWEENEY: Research always continues.

PRESIDENT: Then the deployment of the gas to Brazil was all in the line of research?

SWEENEY: That is correct.

PRESIDENT: Who ordered the deployment?

No response.

SWEENEY: I didn't, sir.

PRESIDENT: Secretary Parson?

PARSON: An investigation within the department of defense is underway on that, sir.

PRESIDENT: You don't know who sent the gas to Brazil?

PARSON: I know I didn't.

PRATT: I didn't either.

PRESIDENT: We must know the facts. We must be able to protect ourselves. General Pratt, do you have any idea who ordered this deployment? (*Long pause.*) Any idea at all?

PRATT: I do not.

PRESIDENT (*sighs*): Well, what do we do to extricate ourselves? (*Long pause as* PRESIDENT *turns to each of his advisors.*)

PARSON: In matters involving the national security—

COLE: We have the right to withhold certain information—

SWEENEY: CB97 is a comparatively humane—

STILES: We could say *they* used the gas on *us*.

COLE: The Brazilians? We couldn't make it stick.

STILES: Why not? The Russians supplied them.

> COLE *shakes his head.*

The Chinese?

PRESIDENT: One foreign crisis at a time, Tim, please.

STILES: The Russians will understand. They know American politics.

COLE: I don't see any way out of conceding deployment.

PARSON: If we concede deployment, there goes your ball game.

COLE: Not if intelligence reports led us to suspect the Brazilians were in the process of being supplied with nerve gas.

STILES: Isn't that what I said?

COLE: I'm not finished. We could not risk the safety of our command by overlooking these reports, so strictly as a deterrent—to keep them from using their gas on *us*—deployment of CB97 was ordered.

PRATT: This could very well be the case.

PARSON: I like that. Intelligence reports—

COLE: And captured enemy documents.

STILES: But then what? Do they use it and we responded, or what?

PRATT: Colonel Dawn ordered it.

STILES: He's dead, isn't he? We can't blame it on anybody dead.

COLE: I lean toward a mishap—an accident.

PARSON: Every time we report an accident the military is made to look like fools.

COLE: This won't be blamed on you. A gas leak.

SWEENEY: Our gas doesn't leak!

COLE: Well, it's got to be something like a gas leak.

STILES: An act of God.

PARSON: Maybe it was hit by lightning.

PRATT: The rainy season is five months away.

PARSON: Maybe one of the storage tanks gets hit by an enemy shell.

PRATT: That could happen.

SWEENEY: What are CB97 storage tanks doing within the range of enemy shells?

PARSON: All right, say a stray enemy shell.

PRATT: A guerrilla patrol could have gotten behind our lines. That does happen.

COLE: That's very good, General Pratt.

PARSON: Excellent, General Pratt. A suicide patrol. We don't know if they knew what those storage tanks contained and deliberately shelled them or—

COLE: It could have been an accident or deliberate.

PARSON: We'll never know. No one will ever know.

STILES: That's it! By golly, that does it!

SWEENEY: It does seem the simplest way.

PRESIDENT: Now that we know what happened, how do we release it?

Lights fade on President's office.

act one

scene five

Lights up on battlefield. An eerie blue light. CUTLER *and* WEEMS *are staggering across battlefield.*

CUTLER: My face feels funny.

WEEMS: Mine too.

CUTLER: Kind of soft and pulpy. I've never been able to breathe so easy.

WEEMS: Me too.

CUTLER: I think the gas has cleared up my sinuses. Whatever becomes of us, Captain, it's classified information. I hope you're aware of that.

WEEMS: But we can talk about it just between the two of us.

CUTLER: Anyone around?

WEEMS: I can't turn my head.

37

CUTLER: I can't either. But where my leg is missing —it feels great.

WEEMS: I never felt better. Let's rest.

He helps CUTLER *to the ground, and lights a cigarette.*

CUTLER: What I wouldn't give for a smoke.

WEEMS: It's my last. (*He continues to smoke.*)

CUTLER: Whatever I say to you—it's confidential.

WEEMS: Absolutely.

CUTLER: I've got to tell somebody—and you're a doctor.

WEEMS: This is a privileged communication.

CUTLER: What are you writing down?

WEEMS: I'm not writing down anything.

CUTLER: What's your hand doing in your pocket?

WEEMS *takes his hand out of his pocket.*

You must think I'm crazy.

WEEMS: You're under great stress. There's only one way I know of to relieve great stress. Get it off your chest.

CUTLER: How do I know you are who you say you are?

WEEMS: What's on your mind, Lieutenant?

CUTLER: You could be trying to entrap me!

WEEMS: Why should I want to do that?

CUTLER: Someone has to take the blame for the gas! You could be CIA!

WEEMS *chuckles.*

Sent out to bring me back for court-martial! (*Takes out his 45.*) I'm not going back with you!

WEEMS: I'm not going to leave you here.

CUTLER: You are CIA!

WEEMS: I'm a doctor. You're my patient.

CUTLER: You could be Chico!

WEEMS: I'm an American doctor.

CUTLER: How can I tell? Your uniform's all in shreds!

WEEMS: That's the gas.

CUTLER: I don't know anything about the gas! For Christ's sake, will you leave me alone!

WEEMS: Best to get it off your chest, son.

CUTLER: Are you sure you're not Chico?

WEEMS: I'm an American.

CUTLER: Are you sure you're not CIA?

WEEMS: I'm an American.

CUTLER: Are you sure you're an American?

WEEMS: I'm an American.

CUTLER: Are you sure you're loyal?

WEEMS: I'm a *doctor!*

CUTLER: And you're not going to write down any of what I tell you?

WEEMS (*turns away*): Forget it.

CUTLER: Wait! The gas—

WEEMS (*turns back*): What gas?

CUTLER (*turns away*): The CB97—

> *From his pocket* WEEMS *removes a tiny tape recorder and stretches the mike toward* CUTLER.

The gas—the whole thing was my idea—

> *Lights fade on battlefield.*

act one

scene six

Lights up on President's office.

STILES: Who can we give the story to?

PARSON: Most of the press corps in Washington will play ball.

STILES: This story can't come out of Washington.

COLE: Right. It would be best to come from on the spot. I would think if we could take the accent off the gas and place it on the extremely hazardous nature of these enemy suicide patrols—

PARSON: Yes. And to illustrate—there was this recent incident with the gas— We've worked a lot with these guys in the past; I have no doubt most will be willing to see it our way.

PRESIDENT: Make up a press list, Secretary Parson, and let me review it.

PARSON: Yes, sir.

PRESIDENT: Say in fifteen minutes?

PARSON: Right.

PRESIDENT: Tim, we might want to follow this up by a story out of Washington. A backgrounder with someone we can trust.

STILES: Do you want a list?

PRESIDENT (*tired*): Yes. Everybody go inside and make up a list.

PARSON, COLE, *and* STILES *rise.*

In the meantime you, Professor Sweeney, can write down a simplified history of the CB97: when it was developed, what it is, its humane properties, et cetera.

SWEENEY *nods.*

In fifteen minutes.

PRESIDENT *sighs.* SWEENEY *rises.*

General Pratt—um—General Pratt, it seems to me there is still a trace of confusion in your story. I'd like you to go over it again in your mind. See what you can come up with. All right?

PRATT: Yes, sir.

PRESIDENT (*indicates stage left*): You can use that office. Mr. Stiles will show you.

STILES *helps him, and returns.*

Well, what do we do with him?

STILES: We can't let the press at him.

COLE: We can put him away in a hospital.

SWEENEY: He can resign for reasons of ill health.

STILES: He can't resign.

PARSON: It'll look bad.

COLE: He has to be promoted.

PARSON: To clear the air.

COLE: Maybe a White House ceremony in his honor.

STILES: Good! We give him a new medal.

PARSON: He has every medal.

STILES: We give him a presidential citation.

COLE: And a new job.

PARSON: You can't just kick him upstairs.

STILES: Where do we put him?

PARSON: West Point?

COLE: We don't want him too far away.

PARSON: Draft director?

PRESIDENT: I have been thinking for some time of forming a Presidential Task Force on Problems of the Domestic Economy in the Year 2000. I had in mind the Secretary of State as chairman. Perhaps General Pratt should have the job instead.

General murmur of assent. PRESIDENT *rises. Others rise.*

Gentlemen, I do not want to keep you from your lists.

They exit stage right. PRESIDENT *sits heavily. After a moment, a low murmur.*

Dear God. (*Switches on intercom.*) You can come in now, Evelyn.

He sits back and waits. MRS. HALE *enters through door behind President's desk. She stands and waits.*

Evelyn, I'm going to tell you the truth about what's happened, but I want your promise of utmost secrecy. I don't want this leaked to any of your pet peace groups. Do I have your promise?

MRS. HALE: You can leak, but I can't.

PRESIDENT: I happen to be President.

MRS. HALE: Then don't confide in me.

PRESIDENT: If I didn't confide in you, you'd be impossible to live with. Besides, you make an accurate barometer for a certain kind of public opinion.

MRS. HALE: What kind?

PRESIDENT: The nineteenth-century kind. Those who see our problems as solvable.

MRS. HALE: Why are you so bitter toward me? Is it because you know you're wrong and I'm right?

PRESIDENT: At least that's an explanation you can accept. I wish you had a little more understanding for the burdens of my office.

MRS. HALE: I can't listen to any more about the

"Agony of Power." I still remember how much more agony you were in when you were out of power.

PRESIDENT: You always mock me.

MRS. HALE: You never listen to me!

PRESIDENT: Most of Washington thinks I listen too much to you.

MRS. HALE: Washington!

PRESIDENT: Why do you hate Washington? Because I'm its first citizen?

MRS. HALE: I hate it because it's unreal. Stop feeling sorry for yourself.

PRESIDENT: Am I unreal?

MRS. HALE: You don't exist. Nobody here exists. That's what scares me most about Washington. All these absent people making war.

PRESIDENT: You're angry because I didn't name you Secretary of State.

MRS. HALE: You treat me as a joke.

PRESIDENT: I treat you—I treat you at arm's length. It's the closest I can come to you these days.

MRS. HALE: How can I shut up when I know you're wrong?

PRESIDENT (*sarcastic*): That's more than I have a right to expect. But I do expect you to play by the rules of the game! It's in here that we thrash out our differences. Out there we present a united front.

MRS. HALE: What happened in Brazil?

PRESIDENT: You'll play by the rules?

No response.

Is that agreed?

MRS. HALE: First tell me what happened in Brazil.

PRESIDENT (*suddenly businesslike*): Recent intelligence reports and captured enemy documents revealed to us that the Chinese were supplying or were about to supply the Brazilians with a quantity of deadly nerve gas. As a deterrent action, we warned the Brazilians that we were deploying the chemical Nerve Agent CB97 to our forces in the field to be used *only* in the event of a gas attack on the part of the enemy. The enemy knew this. They were warned. In a night patrol action of two nights ago enemy forces infiltrated the area where our CB97 was stockpiled. An enemy shell hit one of the storage tanks. The nerve gas was released. Seven hundred and fifty of our men were killed. Ninety were paralyzed. You and I both know in how many ways this story can be distorted, made to look very different from what it is—and the meeting, this morning's meeting, was to decide whether, six weeks before an election, we dared release such news.

MRS. HALE: And what did you decide?

PRESIDENT: By unanimous decision, it was agreed that the American people must be told the truth.

MRS. HALE: As you have told it to me.

PRESIDENT: Yes. Channeled through reliable sources. There must be no leaks. Well?

MRS. HALE: Well what?

PRESIDENT: What do you think?

MRS. HALE: I think I want a divorce.

PRESIDENT: Christ! Evelyn—behave.

MRS. HALE: You've become as dishonest with me as you are with the rest of the country. I don't have to swallow these lies! I am your wife, not your constituent! I want a divorce!

PRESIDENT: Don't make me lose respect for you.

MRS. HALE: The arrogance! You're not going to get away with this! Even the pollsters know we're not winning this war! Why should the Brazilians, in a war they're winning, import, into their own country, poison gas!

PRESIDENT: No one said they were importing it. You're too self-righteous to listen to anybody who isn't carrying a picket sign. What I said was *unconfirmed* intelligence reports—

MRS. HALE: And captured enemy documents!

PRESIDENT: What's wrong with captured enemy documents?

MRS. HALE: They only get captured after we've written them! You'll never be able to explain why we put the gas there unless it was meant to be used! To be *experimented* with! Is that what really happened? Your experiment backfired?

PRESIDENT: It wasn't my experiment!

MRS. HALE: Sweeney's experiment!

PRESIDENT: Other husbands get support from their wives. Why can't I?

MRS. HALE: I've never stopped supporting your ideals.

PRESIDENT: My ideals haven't changed.

MRS. HALE: Then why these lies?

PRESIDENT: We're at war!

MRS. HALE: I'm not talking about lies to Brazilians— I'm talking about lies to Americans! This is the government of the United States you're running, not an advertising agency!

PRESIDENT: You don't have the vaguest understanding of the processes of change! You make us sound like a gang of conspirators!

MRS. HALE: Well, aren't you? You talk only to each other, accept intelligence only from hired hands, debate the issues only with the insiders, call their guesses a consensus and bury their mistakes because no one but you and your henchmen have the "vaguest understanding of the processes of change"! Well, I won't be a party to it. I won't be your coconspirator!

PRESIDENT: You agreed to play by the rules.

MRS. HALE: One more lie!

PRESIDENT: Not five minutes ago you agreed.

MRS. HALE: You are unbelievable! You believe anything you want to believe!

PRESIDENT (*rises, very cold*): Evelyn, I have work to do.

MRS. HALE (*reaches for phone*): And so do I!

PRESIDENT: Get off that phone.

No response.

Get off that phone!

No response.

That is my phone!

MRS. HALE: Get me The New York Times.

Lights fade on President's office.

Cutler, Weems

act one

scene seven

Lights up on battlefield. An eerie purple light. Cutler's back is to WEEMS, *who is holding out the mike of the tape recorder to pick up Cutler's voice.*

CUTLER: The first thing you got to learn is how to take orders. The second thing you got to learn is how to look good. All your buddies are looking good. You don't want your buddies to see you not looking good. That's how you start. After awhile it gets to be automatic. Like riding a bicycle. The third thing you got to learn is how many you can take with you when you go. You take only one with you, you can hardly call yourself a man. You take from two to five with you, you can call yourself a man but I wouldn't say you look good. You take over five, up to ten, you're looking good. You take over ten, up to eighteen, nineteen—you're looking real good. Anything you take over twenty and upwards says you're all balls. Twenty and upwards. All balls. I know a lot of men in this war who went out looking real good. But I can count on the fingers of one hand the number of men I know who went out all balls. (*Tries to count.*) I can't count on my fingers.

WEEMS: What's wrong?

CUTLER (*holds out a rigid hand*): My fingers won't count.

WEEMS *hides tape recorder.*

WEEMS: Let me have a look.

Begins to massage Cutler's fingers.

CUTLER: You must think I'm a real shit, pulling a gun on you. You know how many times I've been wounded in action? Six times. Losing my leg is seven.

WEEMS: I'm sorry.

CUTLER: What?

WEEMS: Three fingers broke off.

CUTLER: You did your best. Losing my fingers is eight.

WEEMS: It doesn't hurt?

CUTLER: Other things hurt. Not my fingers.

WEEMS: Where does it hurt?

CUTLER: It hurts knowing I'm not going to go out all balls. It hurts knowing I'm not going to go out so much as looking real good—or even plain good. All the guys I'm taking with me when I go are my own guys. You want me to worry about three fingers?

WEEMS: You're quite a man, Lieutenant.

CUTLER: I'm not a man.

WEEMS: You are a man. I'm the one who's not a man.

CUTLER: I'm not half the man you are. You came out here to get me.

WEEMS: I came out here to turn you in. I'm not a man. I'm CIA.

CUTLER: You're a doctor.

WEEMS: I'm not a doctor. I'm responsible for your losing a leg and three fingers.

CUTLER: You were doing your job.

WEEMS: My job was to get you to confess and bring you back for court-martial.

CUTLER: You're doing your job, aren't you? To me, that's a real man.

WEEMS: I'm not a man, I'm a shit.

CUTLER: Being a shit is part of being a man. You're looking good.

WEEMS: You don't want to shoot me?

CUTLER (*holds out his hand*): With what?

WEEMS: I'm going to burn my notes.

> WEEMS *rips notes out of his pocket and ignites them with a cigarette lighter.* CUTLER *grabs them out of his hand and beats out the flames.*

Don't!

WEEMS *tries to rise, but cannot.* CUTLER *crawls away from him.*

I can't get up!

CUTLER: I'm going to sign these notes!

WEEMS: Don't do it!

CUTLER *laboriously signs notes with his mutilated hand as* WEEMS *drags himself toward him.*

CUTLER: Shit! Nobody will believe this is my signature.

WEEMS: I'm going to bust up this goddamn tape recorder! (*He smashes tape recorder.*)

CUTLER: It don't matter! I got the notes!

WEEMS: Anybody who tells me you're not all balls will have to settle with me.

CUTLER: Same here.

WEEMS: What's your first name, Cutler?

CUTLER: George. My buddies all call me Buzz. What's yours?

WEEMS: Richard. My buddies call me Rick.

They slowly begin to crawl closer, their hands reaching out to each other. As they crawl, the lights go up in the President's office. Neither the PRESIDENT *nor* MRS. HALE *has moved since their last scene.*

MRS. HALE (*on phone*): Get me The New York Times.

PRESIDENT *turns and stalks out through door behind desk.* MRS. HALE *glares after him.*

Yes, I'm holding.

Lights go out in President's office. The sound of scuffling. A pained gasp.

No!

A low groan. A pause, during which CUTLER *and* WEEMS *reach each other and shake hands.*

Lights up in President's office to reveal MRS. HALE *lying prostrate and bleeding across President's desk. In her chest, embedded like a stake, is a picket sign reading "Make Love Not War."*

CUTLER: You can let go of my hand now, Rick.

WEEMS: You'd think so, wouldn't you? But I can't.

> *Lights fade on battlefield.*
> *Lights fade on President's office.*

Staff with General Pratt

President Hale, Mrs. Hale

TOP LEFT: *In the President's office*

Confrontation

The Murder Weapon

act two

scene one

SWEENEY, COLE, STILES, PARSON *sit around President's desk as before. They are tense, pale, and shift about in their chairs uncomfortably.*

SWEENEY (*under his breath*): Unbelievable.

PARSON (*under his breath*): Hell of a business.

COLE (*under his breath*): I didn't like her, but—

STILES (*under his breath*): It looks bad—

> PRESIDENT *enters. All rise as he crosses to his desk. From behind desk, still standing—*

PRESIDENT (*hoarsely*): My wife— (*Clears throat.*) Mrs. Hale passed away fifteen minutes ago. She never regained consciousness.

> *Chorus of overlapping condolences which* PRESIDENT *abruptly puts an end to by sitting down.*

59

Please. (*He motions for them to be seated.*) I'm aware of what you thought of her. Sweeney, you were fond of her—a little, I think. The rest of you. Well—I doubt if there's an accusation you didn't make behind her back that I didn't make to her face. Well, we all underrated her. She was the best part of me. My moral center. Now that she is gone, I have little heart left for this job. I am speaking to you from the heart now. From the heart. But the President is also the Commander in Chief. I can no more allow myself to falter in the White House—

PRATT *enters, stumbles to his seat.*

than General Pratt here can allow himself to falter in the field. And so to business. Gentlemen, an assassin has achieved access to the inner chamber of the President of the United States. If he has struck once, nothing prevents him from striking again. And again. None of us is safe until he has been apprehended. In order to avert national hysteria, we will delay an announcement of Mrs. Hale's death until this crime is solved and an explanation decided upon for the American people. But there are bound to be leaks. That gives us only a few hours. Mr. Attorney General . . .

COLE: Yes, Mr. President.

PRESIDENT: Please bring in the murder weapon.

Hum of excitement in room as COLE *exits stage right and returns carrying picket sign with pointed, bloody stump.*

Lift it up so we can get a look at it.

STILES (*reads*): "Make Love Not War."

PARSON: The bastards! Sorry, Mr. President.

PRESIDENT: Do any of you gentlemen remember seeing this particular picket sign before?

PARSON: We see plenty of signs like that at the Pentagon. Thousands.

STILES: We've all seen signs like that.

Chorus of assent.

PRESIDENT: What can you tell us about this sign, Mr. Cole?

COLE: I've had a fingerprint check made, Mr. President. We have found two very clear sets of prints.

STILES: Well, there we are!

PRESIDENT: Have these prints been identified?

COLE: Yes, sir.

Hands PRESIDENT *envelope. He removes paper from envelope and reads it.*

PRESIDENT: One set of fingerprints belongs to Mr. Cole.

Others gasp, turn sharply to COLE.

The second set of fingerprints belongs to me.

Others gasp, turn sharply to PRESIDENT. *Murmurs of dissent.*

My prints and your prints.

Lights fade on President's office.

Accusation

act two

scene two

Lights up on battlefield. Eerie orange light. CUTLER *and* WEEMS *are stretched out, holding hands.*

WEEMS: I smell something.

CUTLER: Gas?

WEEMS: I think it's bodies.

CUTLER: Bodies smell worse than that. I don't mind this smell.

WEEMS (*inhales deeply*): It's not bad. I've never been able to breathe so easy. I've lost the power to blink.

CUTLER: How do you know?

WEEMS: Because I can't blink. Can you?

CUTLER: I try not to blink. You miss things. Besides,

you know you can blink if you want to, don't you?

WEEMS: I guess I do.

CUTLER: Even if we don't know, we still know. Inside we know.

WEEMS: I always felt I could do anything if I wanted to.

CUTLER: That's what makes us strong.

WEEMS: I just don't want to.

CUTLER: That's what we mean by freedom.

WEEMS: I feel more free right now than I've ever felt in my life.

CUTLER: Because of self-control. There's a joy in doing, but there's also a joy in not doing. And that can be a richer joy.

WEEMS: When you make the disadvantages—what everybody says are disadvantages—advantages.

CUTLER: You can even be a slave and be free.

WEEMS: If you want to be.

CUTLER: Right!

WEEMS: I don't care what anybody says, I like this smell.

CUTLER: It's all in what you're used to.

WEEMS: How can we be so certain bodies are such a bad smell? Like a rose is supposed to be a good smell. But what about rose fever? We're brainwashed.

CUTLER: Nothing's as bad as you're afraid it's going to turn out to be.

WEEMS: You know the way we are now? Holding hands?

CUTLER: It doesn't hurt anymore.

WEEMS: Listen, Buzz. What if you and me, our hands locked, is the next stage?

CUTLER: Next stage of what?

WEEMS: Evolution. Everybody joined together. Maybe the way we've been all our lives isn't natural. That this is natural. The way we are now. You and me and whoever comes along— a rescue squad—they take our hands, and their hands get locked into our hands, and a squad of Chicos comes along and they see this squad of guys holding hands. You think they'll shoot? They won't be able to shoot. Because it's the wave of the future. They'll take our hands. And more and more guys come along—their side and our side—gooks and colored guys—they'll see this daisy chain—in the middle of a war zone. This beautiful, peace-loving daisy chain, and they'll drop their guns. It will sound like a very loud bomb, the sound of all those guns dropping at one time. And they'll join hands with our hands so that there's no reason to fight anymore because we're all one body with these millions of held hands. No more outsiders. Just one enormous insider.

A pause. Neither man moves. CUTLER *inhales deeply.*

CUTLER: Like a field of clover. (*Inhales deeply.*)

WEEMS: What do you think, Buzz?

CUTLER: It looks good. (*Inhales deeply.*) I'm getting high.

Lights fade on battlefield.

act two

scene three

Lights up on President's office.

PRESIDENT: Do you wish to confess, Mr. Cole?

COLE: No, sir.

PRESIDENT: Neither do I. Let's have a closer look.

> COLE *hands* PRESIDENT *picket sign.*

I always assumed these supports were made of wood. This one is steel.

SWEENEY: Steel!

PRESIDENT: What do you make of this, Secretary Parson? (*Hands sign to* PARSON.)

PARSON: Ordinary cardboard placard. Steel support. Stapled. Sweeney? (*Passes it to* SWEENEY, *who freezes.*)

SWEENEY: I don't want to touch it.

PARSON *shrugs and passes it to* STILES.

STILES: How could anyone smuggle anything this size into the White House?

PRESIDENT: Good question.

STILES *passes sign to* PRATT.

PRATT: Thank you. (*Feels rod.*) Ouch. This tip is jagged. As if it's been broken off.

COLE (*crosses and takes sign from* PRATT): He's right. Something else was on here and it's been broken off.

PRESIDENT: We have now examined the murder weapon and made some interesting findings. The support is not wood, but steel. The tip is jagged. Something has been broken off indicating that the original form of this instrument differs from its present form. And Mr. Stiles has brought up the interesting question of how so conspicuous an object was carried into the White House. Let's see if we can do as well with the fingerprints. Mr. Cole?

COLE: The fingerprints were found up here. Behind the placard.

SWEENEY: Behind the placard?!

COLE: About three inches down. The first and clearest set are identified as yours, Mr. President. Your right hand is below your left. Both hands grip the support tightly with both thumbs pointing inward and downward, thus.

PRESIDENT (*rises and demonstrates grip in air*): Is this correct?

COLE: Your left thumb should overlap somewhat into the palm of your right hand.

PRESIDENT: Like this?

COLE: That would be right.

PRESIDENT (*tries a downward stabbing motion*): An awkward method of impaling someone if you happen to be right-handed. And I am right-handed. Now, tell us about your fingerprints, Mr. Cole.

COLE: My prints are not as recent as yours. But they clasp or grip the support in an identical manner.

PRESIDENT: And you are also right-handed.

COLE: Yes, sir.

PRESIDENT: You are not ambidextrous?

COLE: No, sir. You can check my files. In any case, your prints are the more recent ones.

SWEENEY: The whole thing is impossible!

PRESIDENT: What is impossible, Professor Sweeney?

SWEENEY: It's impossible for anyone to grip the support behind the placard with the placard attached.

COLE *offers him the picket sign. He recoils.*

No—try it yourself. There just isn't enough space.

COLE: He's right.

PARSON *takes picket sign from him and tries to grip it.*

PARSON: You can't get your fingers around. (*Hands sign to* STILES.)

STILES (*refuses sign*): I trust you. So what does that prove?

SWEENEY: Both sets of fingerprints had to be on the support *before* the placard was stapled on.

PRATT: Before the murder.

SWEENEY: Exactly!

STILES: Fingerprints can be planted.

PRESIDENT: No, I don't think these prints were planted.

SWEENEY: But how did they get there?

PRESIDENT: Take a closer look at the support, won't you, Mr. Cole. Does it look familiar?

COLE: No, sir.

PRESIDENT: That's because you're still looking at it as a picket sign. Try to imagine some sort of appendage on the jagged tip.

COLE: No, I have never seen this before.

PRESIDENT: Does anyone else see anything?

PARSON (*slowly*): Yes.

PRESIDENT: What?

PARSON *shakes his head.*

Professor Sweeney?

SWEENEY: I have many ideas. I'm sorting them out.

PRESIDENT: Mr. Stiles?

>STILES *shakes his head.*

Mr. Cole, I believe you said this morning that those were your golf clubs in the anteroom. Would you go out there and bring back your driver?

COLE (*doesn't move*): Are you suggesting that's my driver? (*Takes picket sign in his hands.*) It is my driver. (*Looks at* PRESIDENT, *stricken.*) Oh, my God! It's my driver! (*Collapses in his chair.*) It's my driver—it's my driver—

PARSON: I had a hunch!

SWEENEY: Of course! You said this morning that you couldn't resist taking a few practice swings with —with—

PRESIDENT: Mr. Cole's driver.

SWEENEY: Was that it? I don't play golf.

PRESIDENT: Do you remember my saying that, Mr. Cole?

COLE: Yes, sir. But my driver—

PRESIDENT: Do you remember, Secretary Parson?

PARSON: I don't think I do, Mr. President.

PRESIDENT: Mr. Stiles?

STILES: You said it all right. I was sitting right here.

PRESIDENT: You were not in the room at the time, General Pratt.

PRATT: No, sir.

PARSON: I remember now! I do remember.

PRESIDENT: Well, we have come a long way in a short time. We now know that the murder weapon was no ordinary picket sign, but the shaft of a golf club with the head broken off. This explains the fingerprints. Now, what else have we learned? We have learned that the murderer went to considerable trouble to make sure that the President's fingerprints would be found on the murder weapon.

PARSON: A frame-up!

SWEENEY: But how could he hope to get away with it?

PRESIDENT: Obviously he couldn't hope to get away with it. He hoped to interfere with—possibly even to halt this investigation. For those prints represent two things. They represent a confession.

SWEENEY: A confession?

PRESIDENT: And they represent a warning.

SWEENEY *and* PARSON: A *warning!*

PRESIDENT: A confession and a warning. The murderer is confessing that he knew my fingerprints were on that golf club and he is warning me that the only way he could know this was to be seated in one of these chairs when I mentioned to Mr. Cole that I had my hands on his driver this morning.

COLE: Mr. President?

PRESIDENT: Mr. Cole?

COLE: Should we pursue this course? Is it wise?

STILES: There must be some other explanation.

Others in short outbursts of agitated ad lib comments.

PRESIDENT (*slams his hand on desk*): You think I'm pursuing this for personal reasons? Once a Pandora's box of fear and doubt is left lying open in our midst, we will, every one of us, be sucked helplessly into its maw.

COLE: If I may offer a dissenting view?

PRESIDENT: I am most anxious to hear it.

COLE: First of all, Mr. President, I want to say how remarkably I think you've conducted this entire business.

Others murmur assent. PRESIDENT *nods in acceptance of compliment.*

Mrs. Hale's death was an error. No doubt about it. Some one of us panicked. But whichever one of us he is, there can be no question that he had only his country's interests at heart. His motive was misguided, possibly half-mad, but rooted in a love for this country that the First Lady did not share, rooted in a belief in the continuity of this administration, *your* administration, that the First Lady tried unceasingly to divide. I'm not defending the brutal slaying of your wife, Mr. President, I know how dear she was to you.

But the Pandora's box of fear and doubt you so eloquently speak of cannot be nailed shut by conducting a witch hunt among your advisors. And make no mistake. A witch hunt this investigation must inevitably become: replete with rumor, lie, half-truth, and innuendo. By this route, we will destroy ourselves more successfully than our worst enemies dream.

PRESIDENT: You suggest we drop this investigation?

COLE: In the interests of national security, I do, sir.

PRESIDENT (*coldly*): We are speaking of my wife, Mr. Cole, not some Brazilian. We will proceed with our investigation. Mr. Cole, Mr. Parson, Mr. Stiles, Professor Sweeney, General Pratt: this morning, before, during, or after our meeting, did any of you see anything or hear anything on the part of anyone else in this room that in the light of later events demands clarification?

A stony response.

Mr. Cole, where were you at the time of the murder?

COLE: You seriously want me to answer that question?

PRESIDENT: You are free to seek the advice of counsel.

COLE (*coldly*): You know where I was. Where we all were. Out in the anteroom putting together a list of trustworthy newsmen to whom we could break the Brazilian suicide night patrol story.

PRESIDENT: You were all there?

All nod.

At no time did any of you leave?

All shake their heads.

At no time did any of you see any of the others leave?

All shake their heads.

That puts you in sort of a difficult position, doesn't it, General Pratt? You weren't with the others.

PRATT: No, sir.

PRESIDENT: You were alone.

PRATT: I'm a blind, half-paralyzed man, Mr. President.

PRESIDENT: An old night fighter, as you described yourself.

PRATT: I wasn't in the room when you talked about golf.

PRESIDENT: That is true.

PRATT: Besides, I wasn't alone for the whole time.

PRESIDENT: You weren't?

PRATT: Someone opened the door.

PRESIDENT: Who opened the door?

PRATT: Someone opened it and must have seen the room was occupied. Anyhow, he closed it right away.

PRESIDENT: Do you know who it was?

PRATT: He mumbled something like "Sorry." I didn't quite get it.

PRESIDENT: Would you recognize the voice if you heard it again?

PRATT: I have sharp ears.

PRESIDENT: Mr. Cole, will you say "Sorry" for General Pratt.

COLE: Sorry.

PRATT: It was more of a mumble.

COLE (*mumbles*): Sorry.

PRATT: That could be it.

COLE: I wasn't in there!

PRESIDENT: All in good time, Mr. Cole. Secretary Parson, will you mumble "Sorry"?

PARSON: Sorry.

PRATT: I didn't hear it.

PRESIDENT: A louder mumble if you please, Secretary Parson.

PARSON: Sorry.

PRATT: That could be it.

PRESIDENT: Professor Sweeney. Your turn.

SWEENEY: Sorry.

PRESIDENT: In your normal voice, Professor Sweeney.

SWEENEY: That was my normal voice.

PRESIDENT: No, it wasn't. You used a bit of a falsetto.

SWEENEY: I didn't realize, I'm sorry.

PRATT: That's the one! That's it!

SWEENEY: It wasn't me! I didn't go in there!

PRATT: That was your "Sorry"! I'd bet on it.

SWEENEY: I never went into that room! I went into another room!

PRESIDENT: You what?

SWEENEY: To use the telephone! You wanted me to do an on-the-spot description of the CB97. I had to call the office to get some information! But I didn't open General Pratt's door! And I didn't say "Sorry"!

PRATT: That's it!

PRESIDENT: But you did make a phone call!?

SWEENEY: Only for a minute.

PRESIDENT: Why did none of you report that Professor Sweeney left the room to make a telephone call?

PARSON: I guess I didn't see him leave. I was on the phone.

PRESIDENT: In the anteroom?

PARSON: No, Stiles was on the anteroom phone, so I went down the hall and found an empty office.

PRESIDENT: Mr. Stiles?

STILES: I swear I thought they were all there. You know me when I get on the phone.

PRESIDENT: And where were you through all this,

Mr. Cole? Sitting there unnoticed? Perhaps toy-
ing with your golf clubs?

COLE: I was on the phone.

PRESIDENT: Which phone?

COLE: I had to go upstairs to the Lincoln Room.
Stiles, Sweeney, and Parson had all the down-
stairs phones tied up.

PRESIDENT: Did you check the office General Pratt
was in to see if he was on the phone?

COLE: No. And I didn't say "Sorry."

PRATT: That could be it.

PRESIDENT: So any one of you had the opportunity to
remove the driver from the golf bag—

PRATT: I didn't know about it.

PRESIDENT: Except General Pratt.

SWEENEY: I don't play golf. I wouldn't recognize a
driver if it hit me. I mean—

PRESIDENT: Except General Pratt and Professor
Sweeney.

COLE: *If* Sweeney's telling the truth about not play-
ing golf.

SWEENEY: I'm sure the Justice Department will have
it in its files.

COLE: Don't think I won't check.

PRESIDENT: Careful, Mr. Cole.

COLE: I'm sorry, Mr. President. But this is just the
sort of mutual distrust I warned you against.

PRESIDENT: *Warned* me? *Warned* the President! I want you to know something. All of you. How disappointed I am. How grievously disappointed. How my trust in all of you—all of you has been shaken by your refusal to cooperate. Your truculence—

PARSON: Mr. President. If I could say a few words?

PRESIDENT, *suppressing his anger, nods curtly.*

I'm terribly worried the way this thing is going. I don't think it has to go that way. It seems to me we can turn this tragedy into an opportunity. Too often in the past we're the victims of events, and it looks like today we're that all over again. We're in a rough war. And morale isn't what it should be. It's flagging. And one reason morale is flagging is because of lack of support back home. It's a factor our enemies bank on. They know they can't beat us in the field, but they can beat us in our own backyards. That's because our wars aren't real to the people. The people see them on TV, and it's like just another show. I've read some research on this, and it's a fact. So what I say is this: if we could bring this war home to the people, strengthen homefront support, why, it would mean all the difference in the world. So that's the question: do we go on and let events push us around or do we use our initiative and take control of our destinies instead of vice versa?

PRESIDENT: I'm sorry but I don't understand what you're saying.

PARSON: My recommendation, Mr. President, is that the First Lady was assassinated by a suicide squad of Brazilian terrorists.

Lights fade on President's office.

act two

scene four

Lights up on battlefield. An eerie yellow light.

CUTLER: You want to see a fantastic sight? Can you raise up a little?

WEEMS: I think so.

CUTLER: Look at our two hands over there.

WEEMS: How'd they get over there?

CUTLER: They must have rolled over.

WEEMS: I don't remember them breaking off, do you?

CUTLER: That's what's so great about it. Like it's perfectly normal.

WEEMS: Like a new form of birth.

CUTLER: That's just what I was thinking. All the hands in the world becoming one hand.

WEEMS: And ours are the first two. Look at them grip each other.

81

CUTLER: They don't need us.

WEEMS: They need each other.

CUTLER: To them, they're us.

WEEMS: Are we still us?

CUTLER: We're part of us. We always will be.

WEEMS: But the main part—

CUTLER: The main part. Who can say what the main part is?

WEEMS: I've never felt so—I don't know.

CUTLER: What?

WEEMS: It sounds funny to say it—so all together. My leg is coming loose.

CUTLER: Throw it over with my leg.

WEEMS: I can't see your leg. I can't really see too well anymore. And I'm having trouble talking.

CUTLER: I don't have any trouble understanding.

WEEMS: Does my voice sound funny to you?

CUTLER: It sounds more like what you're really about.

WEEMS: I'm getting down to roots.

CUTLER: That's what I mean.

WEEMS: Look what just came off. (*Holds object over his head.*)

CUTLER: I can't see too good either. What is it?

WEEMS: My pecker. I was scratching it, and it came off.

CUTLER: You think there's a secret?

WEEMS: Not anymore.

Lights fade on battlefield.

act two

scene five

Lights up on President's office. Exactly as before.

COLE: It won't work.

STILES: Maybe. But it's in the right direction. Finally we're beginning to get somewhere.

PARSON: Why won't it work?

COLE: We can't blame everything that goes wrong on Brazilian suicide squads.

PARSON: So why not let them have this one and find somebody else for the CB97?

COLE: Because the CB97 is too far along.

SWEENEY: The decision has been made.

PARSON: I'm for making a switch. It's got to be something like a Brazilian suicide squad if we want the American people to get behind this war.

83

COLE: Why can't we make it be Communists? Or a peace group?

STILES: I don't care who we have do it. But one thing I'm strong on. We can't have her killed in the White House.

PARSON: Why not?

STILES: Not six weeks before election. It makes us look ineffectual.

COLE: Stiles is right. She's got to be killed somewhere else.

SWEENEY: But where?

COLE: Tim, where are we most in trouble?

STILES: In the cities, according to Gallup.

COLE: So we're not risking very much if we have her killed in New York?

STILES: New York, Chicago, San Francisco. Doesn't matter.

COLE: We may even pull a sympathy vote.

STILES: For a sympathy vote, I'd scratch New York. Better make it Chicago.

PARSON: There are lots of Communists in Chicago. Can't we do something with that?

STILES: I'd like to help you out on this morale business, Biff, but the more I look at it, the less likely it seems.

COLE: Let's not forget the picket sign.

SWEENEY: "Make Love Not War."

COLE: I favor a peace group.

PRATT: Or students.

PARSON: Why not make it the blacks?

STILES: Chicago's full of them.

SWEENEY: Why always look for left-wing villains? Why not pick on the Birch Society?

PARSON: Come off it, Sweeney. The Birch Society? "Make Love Not War"?

SWEENEY: I just don't see why everyone has to pick on the left. Anyhow, no one will believe they did it. She was antiwar, pro-Negro, and pro-student.

STILES: He's right. No one will believe it.

PARSON: I think they'll believe it.

PRATT: It could very easily be the Negroes.

STILES: You're out of touch. It's out of the question.

COLE: So who did it?

SWEENEY: Why does she have to have been murdered?

STILES: That's very good, Sweeney.

COLE: An accident?

PARSON: A plane crash?

SWEENEY: A car crash?

PRATT: A hunting accident?

PARSON: A fatal illness.

PRATT: Pneumonia?

COLE: Takes too long.

PRATT: Cancer?

STILES: Bad image.

COLE: And it takes too long.

PARSON: A heart attack!

SWEENEY: I know! Food poisoning!

COLE: Food poisoning—

PARSON: Food poisoning—

STILES: I like it!

PRATT: Food poisoning in Chicago. It could have happened.

SWEENEY (*proudly*): What do you think, Mr. President?

PRESIDENT: What do I think? What do I *think!* I think you people aren't human. This is my wife you're talking about. Will you listen to yourselves? The First Lady! Do you have the slightest notion of what you sound like? A human being. She was a human being! This sounds like a madhouse! One of you has murdered a flesh-and-blood woman and not a single one of you cares! What have you done to your humanity?

Embarrassed pause.

COLE: If you pardon me for saying so, Mr. President, I think you're oversimplifying. I fully sympathize with your feelings—

PARSON: We all do.

COLE: And we stand in awe of the remarkable manner in which you've conducted this investigation —thus far.

PRATT: But we have to be realists.

COLE: We must be realists. That doesn't mean we lack human feeling or a sense of compassion.

PRATT: We do not lack human feeling.

COLE: But there is a difference between how a feeling man may act in public life and how he may act in private life.

SWEENEY: We in public life have the most difficult burden of all.

PARSON: It is our job to protect the national interest.

SWEENEY: It is our job to get things done.

COLE: It is our job to do what's best.

PRATT: That doesn't mean we're not human.

SWEENEY: Every action we recommend is on behalf of humanity.

PARSON: Only the enemies of humanity will gain by our differences.

SWEENEY: It's very complicated.

COLE: We cannot afford to oversimplify.

PRATT: America would be destroyed.

PRESIDENT: I'd like to get this straight so that there is no chance later for confusion. It is your unanimous recommendation—am I correct?—that the First Lady did not die in the White House—

OTHERS: Yes—yes—that is correct—

PRESIDENT: That she was not murdered.

OTHERS: No—not murdered—impossible—

PRESIDENT: That somehow, somewhere she died—someway—

OTHERS: Yes—Yes—Yes—

PRESIDENT: An accident—

OTHERS: Very good!—Good!—Good!—

PRESIDENT: I will take your recommendation under advisement. In the meantime, we have gone this far with our investigation. I would like to go a little further.

OTHERS (*not quite in chorus*): No!

PRESIDENT: Is it a risk to the national security to discuss these things among ourselves?

OTHERS (*not quite in chorus*): Yes!

PRESIDENT: There are so many risks. We will just have to be brave. We now come to a key point in our investigation. A point brought up earlier by Postmaster General Stiles. How was so conspicuous an object as a picket sign brought into the White House? Now this is a very large placard indeed. No one could smuggle it in under his coat. How did one of you bring it in? Mr. Cole? You have contributed so much already.

No response.

Secretary Parson, you are famous for your attention to detail.

No response.

Professor Sweeney, you constantly astonish me with the creative use you find for your research.

No response.

Mr. Stiles, you are the most pragmatic man in this room full of pragmatic men.

No response.

General Pratt, is the nation's military arm struck mute?

No response.

Well then, I will have to work it out for myself. Let's take a look at this placard. (*He rips it off the support.*) It is too large to fit into any of your briefcases. And it has not been folded. It might have been worn on the inside of a shirt, but that would make one of you move so stiffly it would surely have been noticed. Although, General Pratt, it wouldn't have been noticed on you.

All stare at PRATT.

However, I see how tightly your uniform fits. And this placard is not creased. You are cleared once again, General Pratt. It is a mystery. How do you bring an eighteen by twenty-four placard reading "Make Love Not War" into the White House without someone seeing it? Secretary Parson, would you like to try again?

No response.

You disappoint me, Secretary Parson. I hoped you would answer, "It would not be noticed if I brought it in hidden among my Brazilian war charts."

Others except for PARSON *slowly rise to their feet.* PARSON *and* PRESIDENT *remain seated, exchanging grim stares.*

Lights fade on President's office.

act two

scene six

Lights up on battlefield. An eerie red light. Cutler's and Weems's heads, arms, and bodies lie scattered about the battlefield.

WEEMS: Can you see me, Buzz?

CUTLER: Not anymore.

WEEMS: I can't see anything. Did you see where my head rolled?

CUTLER: No.

WEEMS: I hope it rolled near my hand. I have an itch on my nose.

CUTLER: I can't feel anything.

WEEMS: You think this is dying?

CUTLER: I don't know what it is, but it looks good.

WEEMS: My whole past is passing in front of my eyes, and I don't recognize any of it.

CUTLER: Does it have the Boy Scouts in it?

WEEMS: Yes.

CUTLER: Does it have touch football?

WEEMS: Yes.

CUTLER: Does it have Sunday mornings in church—the family car—self-reliance—the old swimming hole—homemade cooking—beating up the school bully—the girl next door—overcoming disappointment?

WEEMS: Yes.

CUTLER: I think you've got my past. I must have yours.

WEEMS: We've traded our pasts.

CUTLER: We've shared our pasts.

WEEMS: Everybody has the same history. That's the secret.

CUTLER: But nobody knows it.

WEEMS: Nobody knows the secret.

CUTLER: And the ones who find out—they don't talk about it.

WEEMS: Or talk about anything.

CUTLER: Because they know.

WEEMS: They know it all.

CUTLER: So there's no reason—

WEEMS: To talk.

CUTLER: Or be seen.

WEEMS: Or make an impression.

CUTLER: Or anything.

WEEMS: Because knowing is enough.

CUTLER: That's why nobody else knows.

WEEMS: If we did talk about it, what do you think would happen?

CUTLER: I think it'd end all war.

WEEMS: It would end violence.

CUTLER: It would end mental illness.

WEEMS: All men would be brothers.

CUTLER: There'd be universal love.

WEEMS: And equality.

CUTLER: And generosity of feelings.

WEEMS: If they just knew the secret. How does it look?

CUTLER: What?

WEEMS: My past.

CUTLER: It looks real good, Rick. Warm. Human.

WEEMS: Are you positive?

CUTLER: A typical family: sharing hard times but loving your country; rising early in the morning to work the land—your father already out on the field, you and your five brothers gotten out of bed by your mother, a work worn woman with laughing eyes—

WEEMS: That's not my past.

CUTLER: Is your mother's name Consuela?

WEEMS: No.

CUTLER: Did you ever plant coffee as a kid?

WEEMS: You got some Chico's past.

CUTLER: It looks good.

WEEMS: Where could he be?

CUTLER: Out there. Somewhere. You know what that means, Rick?

WEEMS: It means we're all one.

CUTLER: It means I didn't gas only our own guys. I got me a Chico. I got me at least one Chico.

WEEMS: You have his past.

CUTLER: I got one. Maybe more than one!

WEEMS: All of us lying here—exchanging secrets—

CUTLER: Who knows how many? Maybe I got dozens. Maybe I got up to a hundred! A hundred to take with me when I go!

WEEMS: That's not the way to go.

CUTLER: You kidding? All balls isn't the way to go? How many Chicos you taking with you?

WEEMS: You're forgetting what's true, Buzz.

CUTLER: You're jealous!

WEEMS: Chico, you, and me—we're one!

CUTLER: You're one, you fucking flit! Why are you trying to screw me out of my Chicos?

WEEMS: You're losing the secret!

CUTLER: I don't lose any secrets. I keep all secrets. All secrets are classified cosmic!

Weems's head moves toward Cutler's head.

WEEMS: We're all together, Buzz. You've got my hand!

CUTLER: I don't want your faggot hand! You're not a man. You're not an American. You're Chico!

WEEMS: I'm Chico, you're Chico—

CUTLER: Chico!

Cutler's separated arm draws his gun.

WEEMS: We're all—

Cutler's arm fires at the various parts of WEEMS. *Silence.*

CUTLER: Looking good. Looking real good. All balls.

Lights fade on battlefield.

Stiles, President

act two

scene seven

Lights up on President's office. Exactly as before.

STILES: Mr. President.

PRESIDENT (*still staring at* PARSON): Mr. Stiles?

STILES: I have an urgent matter I would like to take up with you. It must be in private.

PRESIDENT (*sarcastic*): We can all be trusted here, Mr. Stiles.

STILES: It must be in private.

PRESIDENT (*turns his stare onto* STILES): Does it have some bearing on this matter?

STILES: I have never been frivolous with your time.

PRESIDENT: Will you gentlemen please wait together in the anteroom. And this time, if you please, no phone calls.

They exit. STILES *sits.*

STILES: I have known you ever since you entered politics.

PRESIDENT: You brought me into politics.

STILES: I wish I could forget it. You're making a damn fool of yourself!

PRESIDENT: Be careful!

STILES: Oh, for Christ's sake, get off your high horse. Emerson, you're in deep trouble and I'm the only one who can bail you out.

PRESIDENT: I don't care about the election. All I care about is that Parson murdered Evelyn.

STILES: He did? How did he?

PRESIDENT: You know how.

STILES: Do I? How did he know she was in here? She didn't come through the anteroom. I was in the anteroom with Parson and I didn't see her come through.

PRESIDENT: She was waiting in my private study. That door. She always waited for me in there.

STILES: So how did Parson know she was in here?

PRESIDENT: He had to know!

STILES: He couldn't know. None of us could. Well, that's not true. One of us could.

PRESIDENT: Who?!

STILES: You could.

PRESIDENT: You're beginning to waste my time.

STILES: Is that why you're so eager to pin this on Parson?

PRESIDENT: Get out.

STILES: You can't deny you had a motive. If she was my wife, I'd have thought very seriously of killing her.

PRESIDENT: I loved Evelyn!

STILES: Ridiculing you in public. Making you a figure of contempt.

PRESIDENT: It's not true!

STILES: She didn't make you a figure of contempt?

PRESIDENT: Oh, that part is true enough. But if that's a motive for murder there'd be a mass slaughter of wives throughout the country.

STILES: Who had a better opportunity to smuggle the placard into the White House than the President?

PRESIDENT: I won't listen to any more of this drivel.

STILES: It's no more drivel than the claptrap you've been feeding us!

PRESIDENT: How could I have gotten my hands on Cole's driver while all of you were in the anteroom?

STILES: We left. You forced that out of us yourself.

PRESIDENT: *You* didn't leave. You were on the phone.

STILES: That's true. I would have seen you.

PRESIDENT: So I couldn't have taken Cole's driver.

STILES: No.

PRESIDENT: And Parson did!

STILES: How could I see you and miss Parson? All right, say he did take the driver. What did he do next? Go into your office, knock off the head of the driver, fish around in his charts for the placard, staple the placard onto the driver, and run your wife through while she's sitting there watching this whole operation?

PRESIDENT: No, he couldn't do it that way.

STILES: Forget Parson! He didn't know she was in there.

PRESIDENT: Then who knew?

STILES: No one knew.

PRESIDENT: No one?

STILES: Not even the murderer. Mrs. Hale was not supposed to be the victim.

PRESIDENT: My God! He was after *me!*

STILES: Yes!

PRESIDENT: But how could anyone possibly confuse—

STILES: The lights had to be off.

PRESIDENT: That's it. The lights. Parson turns off the lights, he gets the placard—

STILES: I told you to forget Parson! How is he going to find the placard with the lights out?

PRESIDENT: Who, besides Parson, could have carried that placard into the White House?

STILES: It didn't have to be carried in. It could have gotten in some other way.

PRESIDENT: There is no other way!

STILES: The U.S. mails.

PRESIDENT: It was mailed?

STILES: Why not? The murderer mailed it—say a couple of days ago. He could have even included the stick—but having the President's fingerprints on the murder weapon seemed like a better idea. So he mails the placard out in some sort of easily identifiable package, and if he knows anything at all about mail delivery in the White House, he knows it'll be weeks before it's unwrapped. So when he's good and ready, he goes down to the mail room, liberates the placard, swipes the golf club, knocks off the head with one of the tools down in the mail room, and uses the staple gun to affix it to the placard.

PRESIDENT: But why go to all this bother?

STILES: Who does anything simple in Washington?

PRESIDENT: It's impossible! He was bound to be seen in the mail room.

STILES: Let's say he doesn't care if he's seen.

PRESIDENT: But he must care!

STILES: Let's say he doesn't care because he takes it for granted that no one who saw him fooling around in the mail room will ever connect him with the White House murder because nobody but the five of us will ever know about the White House murder. I say five, not six, because you're not supposed to know either. You're supposed to be the victim.

PRESIDENT: It couldn't be covered up!

STILES: The Vice-President is a loyal party member, a dedicated American, and a very ambitious man. No less loyal, dedicated, or ambitious a man than his predecessor. That's you. He would not want to destroy his party, injure his country, and wipe out his chance to be president by placing on trial as an assassin the national chairman of the party.

PRESIDENT: My God, Tim, what are you saying?

STILES: I killed your wife.

PRESIDENT: I don't believe it.

STILES: It was in the dark. She was at your desk, the damned buttinsky. How was I to know? It was a mistake, but maybe it won't matter.

PRESIDENT: My God, it was me you meant to kill! But why? We're friends!

STILES: You were going to lose an election.

PRESIDENT: I wasn't. I would have pulled it out!

STILES: The country is tired of one crisis after another. Last Monday I saw the latest polls and it was crystal clear we were through unless we had a fresh candidate. Somebody not connected to your mistakes.

PRESIDENT: So you planned to assassinate me in the White House.

STILES: Who killed you and where it took place is a technicality. As far as the public was to be concerned, you got it in some other place from a member of the opposition party, who is probably half-crazed and has strong radical sympathies.

PRESIDENT: And that would produce a sympathy vote that would sweep the Vice-President into office.

STILES: That's the scenario.

PRESIDENT: Was the Vice-President in on this plot?

STILES: That dunderhead? He would have panicked.

PRESIDENT: So you plotted and executed this all by yourself.

STILES: That's it.

PRESIDENT: All for the good of the party.

STILES: What's good for the party is good for the country. The party's been my life for forty years. I'm not going to sit by and watch amateurs destroy it.

PRESIDENT: You are referring to me.

STILES: When I recruited you, you had a good image. But you took your wife's advice more seriously than you took mine. Look where it got you.

PRESIDENT: This is startling—startling. I don't know

why, but I can't feel angry. Or vengeful. I must be in shock. You will have to be punished.

STILES: Are you going to have me arrested?

PRESIDENT: Arrested? How can I?

STILES: You seemed pretty eager to spread the truth a little while ago.

PRESIDENT: Among ourselves, yes. Of course! We're equipped to deal with it. But the public—it wouldn't do them any good to hear this sort of thing. It would shake their faith badly. We wouldn't be able to carry on. We've made our share of mistakes, but good Lord, can you imagine those other fellows in power? No, it's vital that we carry on.

STILES (*hands him confession*): I've written out a complete confession. I wrote it in the anteroom before I did it, so cross out your name and stick in your wife's.

PRESIDENT: I don't want it.

STILES: I intend to release it to the press.

PRESIDENT: What are you trying to do to me, Stiles?

STILES: We will not go along as we have in the past.

PRESIDENT: What is it you want?

STILES: A hand in the making of the foreign policy of this government.

PRESIDENT: You're a politician, not a diplomat!

STILES: It's your diplomacy that's destroying our

politics. I'm not going to risk future elections because of your mistakes!

PRESIDENT: I'll consult you as I have in the past.

STILES: No.

PRESIDENT: You won't get any more out of me.

STILES: Then I'll release this confession.

PRESIDENT: You'd destroy the party.

STILES: You haven't left much party for me to destroy.

PRESIDENT: It's a bluff. (*Long exchange of stares.* PRESIDENT *folds.*) What do you want?

STILES: Secretary of Defense.

PRESIDENT: I can't do that to Parson. I've already accused him of murder. I can't take his job away.

STILES: I want Secretary of Defense.

PRESIDENT: I won't do it. Show some human understanding, for God's sake! You want some direction over foreign policy? I'll make you Ambassador to the UN.

STILES: I didn't kill your wife to become an errand boy. Don't treat me with contempt.

PRESIDENT: Ambassador to Brazil.

STILES *glowers.*

Presidential Troubleshooter!

STILES *rises with confession.*

Assistant to the President for Foreign Affairs!

STILES *starts for door.*

The State Department!

STILES (*slowly turns*): You mean it?

PRESIDENT: I have no choice.

STILES (*a slow grin*): Secretary of State.

PRESIDENT: You understand I won't be able to name
you until after the election.

STILES (*beams*): Secretary of State.

PRESIDENT (*rises, crosses to door, and opens it*):
Won't you come in, gentlemen.

Others enter.

First of all, I want to thank all of you for bearing so patiently with me through all of this terrible business. Next, I want to offer my sincerest
apologies to Secretary Parson. Biff knows me
too long and too well not to realize I was not in
my right mind when I made those baseless ac-
cusations. Biff, I beg your understanding and
your forgiveness.

PARSON: Water over the dam.

PRESIDENT: Next. Our attention has been diverted
on the CB97 affair. This was my fault. That
matter should be expedited without further delay. Next— Well, next, I have some unhappy
news of a personal nature. As some of you
may have heard, the First Lady flew quietly to
Chicago last night for a short vacation. I learned
by phone only a few minutes ago that she has

been taken seriously ill. The doctors suspect food poisoning.

Lights up on empty battlefield, the same lights as in President's office. Clouds of gas form over the stage.

OTHERS (*in chorus*): Oh, I'm sorry, Mr. President.

All freeze. The lights turn green.

Curtain

Dick and Jane

dick

and jane

Night in a bedroom. Lights are out. The room is black.

JANE: Not that way— (*Grunts uncomfortably.*)

DICK (*grunts uncomfortably*): Ouch!

JANE: I'm over here.

> DICK *grunts uncomfortably.*

> Wait a minute— (*Grunts.*)

DICK: Will you stop—

> JANE *grunts uncomfortably.*

> Why can't we do it—

JANE: Now where did you go?

> DICK *grunts uncomfortably.*

111

There. There. Perfect. Perfect. Now! Now!

Pause.

DICK: Shit.

JANE: If you'd listen to me—

DICK: Hold it—

JANE: You're moving all wrong.

DICK: Why can't we do it—

JANE: Don't be in such a hurry. I'm not going anywhere. Let me do that.

Pause.

See? I told you to let me—

DICK: Shit.

JANE: I'm over here.

DICK: Hold it—

JANE: That's better.

Pause. A series of grunts by DICK.

You're going too fast.

Slower grunts by DICK.

Faster.

Faster grunts by DICK.

Oh—Ohh—Ohhhhhhhhh—

He pants, out of breath as she sighs happily. A period of silence. Lights go on to reveal: Jane's bedroom; a lamp by the bed; a door leading out into the hall, which is now closed. JANE, *naked, lies under a sheet.* DICK, *his back to* JANE, *is sitting at far edge of bed. He rises and comes around bed. He is fully dressed in a business suit, and is putting on his hat.*

DICK: I have an appointment.

JANE: You have a *what?!* At four in the morning you have a *what?!*

DICK: I have an 8:30 appointment. Have to get crosstown, shower, and shave. Change suits. Eat breakfast. (*Checks his watch.*) Really, it was great. (*Starts toward door.*) It was the best.

JANE: *You bastard!*

DICK (*returns and sits, very formally, at edge of bed*): What can I tell you? It was great. (*Stiffly takes her hand.*) You're the greatest ever. (*Dispassionately takes her in his arms.*) It's you and me all the way, kid.

Both pose lifelessly, then she begins to respond. She pulls him down on top of her, takes off his hat, switches off light. Pause.

JANE: Where are you?

Door opens. Light from hall illuminates DICK *at door, hat on, fully dressed.*

DICK: The greatest. (*He exits. Silence.*)

JANE (*very quiet*): Bastard. (*Long pause. She shouts.*) *You bastard!*

DICK *enters, crosses to Jane's bed, leaving door*

*ajar, so that for a while it remains the only
source of illumination.*

DICK (*sits on edge of bed*): I'll be honest with you,
I'm not getting as much out of this as I expected. I expected, I don't know, a lot more, I
don't know, a lot more, I can't put my finger on
it, I don't know, but you know what I mean, it's
not working out, it's nobody's fault, we've had
some laughs, what the hell, right?

*She stares at him silently. He is increasingly un-
easy.*

I don't care what you call me. You can call me
anything you like. You can think of me any
way you like. That's your problem. It's not my
problem. I go on my merry way.

She continues to stare silently.

You're a bitch, you know that? An aggressive
man-eating bitch! Move this way—that way—
too fast—too slow—up—down—stop—start
— You goddamn traffic cop! Police brutality—
that's what you're guilty of! A maid. I'm nothing
but a maid. I come in three times a week, make
up your body, and go home.

JANE: *Rush* home.

DICK: Why not? It's quitting time, isn't it? After I boff
you, my time is my own.

JANE: To spend on more exotic pleasures.

DICK: I do what I do the best way I know how to do
it, then I go home and enjoy myself.

JANE: And I know how.

DICK: Big deal.

JANE: With your filthy pornography.

DICK: It beats the clean-cut pornography I get around here.

JANE: I'm sorry I can't rise to the level of your fantasy life.

DICK: You could if you wanted to.

JANE: Don't degrade me.

DICK: You're not degraded in my fantasies, you're honored. I honor you.

JANE (*shocked*): You don't use me in your fantasies—

He smiles.

You bastard! I'll sue you!

DICK: When you're not in charge you get very uptight.

JANE: You have no right!

DICK: Now you want to police my fantasies.

JANE: It's *my* person! I should have some rights about the role I play. What's wrong with doing it the regular way?

DICK: My father and mother did it the regular way.

JANE: You're jaded.

DICK: You're dead.

JANE: Not so dead I can't get you aroused anytime I want to.

DICK: Sure you can.

JANE: Sure I can.

DICK: You can't. I fake it.

JANE: You can't fake a hard-on.

DICK: Yes you can.

JANE: You cannot!

DICK: Don't tell me I can't. I do it all the time. If you care enough you can fake anything. Even potency.

She stares, horrified. Her head sinks under the sheet.

I thought you liked to talk afterwards. Isn't that one of your objections—that I'm dressed and out of here before we've had a chance to discuss how good it was? All right, we're talking. Except that's not enough, is it? If I give in to you on talking then the next request is to hold you. If I give in to you on holding the next request is to pet you. Except both of us pet you because you're guiding my hand. And soon the whole damn cycle starts all over again: higher, lower, over here, over there. Baby, I just like to get laid. I didn't bargain for all these extras. And when I have the temerity to suggest a simple little experiment—

JANE: You're sick.

DICK: If it gives me pleasure you tell me it's sick. To you anything more exotic than this way, that way is a perversion. You want to know why I get the hell out of here as fast as I can? Because of tension! This is a very tense bed.

JANE: Not because of me!

DICK: Sure. You're free.

JANE: I *am* free! (*She stares at him in silent challenge.*)

DICK (*starts toward door*): O.K. I'll get my equipment.

JANE: No!

DICK: She's free. What's the point? You don't like fucking, you like talking. You fuck for companionship. I'm a good fucker but a lousy companion. We're incompatible.

JANE: I can't be what I'm not.

DICK: You can't be what you are. I'm trying to free you. (*Reaches for her, she recoils.*) See, how tense you are? (*Puts hand on her neck.*) It's a steel column. I could break rocks on it. Here, let me show you a little exercise. (*Stands on his head.*) Try it. (*She hesitates.*) Come on, try it. It'll relax you.

JANE: What will you be doing?

DICK: Come on, you're making me mad!

JANE: I don't trust you.

DICK (*shouts*): Do we have to fight when I'm standing on my goddamn head? I didn't think it was possible but you make me tense even this way!

JANE, *with great awkwardness, tries a headstand.* DICK *finally rights himself, puts his arms around her legs, and holds her in upside down position.*

Doesn't that feel great?

JANE: Let me down!

DICK *starts to force his head between her legs.*

Let me down, you sick bastard! Help! Rape!

He drops her legs.

DICK: I banish you to permanent slavery! (*Starts to leave.*)

JANE: You want everything all at once. Give me a chance, for Christ's sake!

DICK: You're crying. Why are you crying?

JANE: You make me furious, that's why.

DICK: Then don't cry! Hit!

JANE: What!

DICK: Be free! You hate me. Hit.

JANE *throws her arms behind her back. He struggles with her till he breaks them free. Then, with a wrist lock, he forces her hand to his cheek and slaps it.*

Hit. (*He slaps harder.*) HIT. (*Again.*) Hit. Come on! Like in *your* fantasies.

With her free hand she slugs him, then recoils in horror.

Very good. (*He slaps her hard. She falls.*)

That's not a good fall. Try this. (*He falls.*)
You fall tense. I fall free. Stand up, I'll show you.

JANE: Don't push me.

DICK: I won't push you.

JANE: I want to do it by myself. (*She rises.*)

DICK: That's how you learn.

She staggers, catches herself.

JANE: Wait. (*She staggers again, catches herself.*) I'll get it right this time. (*She stands frozen, trying to fall.*) What's the matter with me? I can't fall! Push me!

DICK: Uh-uh.
He circles her, executing a series of expert falls. She stands frozen.

JANE: Please push me. I can't move.

DICK: You're afraid to make a commitment.

JANE: I'm paralyzed.

DICK: Some people can't handle freedom. You're one of them.

JANE: Help me!

DICK: I can only help those who help themselves.

JANE: That's *God*, you idiot! What are you doing?

He is taking off his clothes.

Dick, I warn you—

He walks toward her. She screams. He passes her and crosses to bed. He picks up her dress, puts it over his head, then starts to get into it.

You maniac! (*She lunges for dress.*)

He turns away from her, throws her his suit.

DICK: Role reversal time!

She drops suit.

Don't crush it! Dammit, put it on! It'll set you free!

JANE (*picks up suit, rips jacket*): You want me to be free? (*Rips sleeve off.*) All right I'm free! (*Rips other sleeve.*) Free! (*Rips trousers.*) Free! (*Throws herself on floor, goes through epilepticlike contortions.*)

DICK *watches, electrified.*

DICK: You've got it!

JANE (*thrashing*): I'm free! I'm free! I'm free! I'm free! I'm free!

DICK (*starts off*): I'll be right back. Stay that way. Don't change! (*Exits.*)

JANE: Free!

DICK (*enters wearing mask, carrying whip in one hand, black leather, high heeled, laced boots in the other. He throws them on bed, exits running. A basketball bounces in. He enters wheeling bicycle, carrying riding crop and watermelon. Basket on bike is filled with paint cans. He parks bike, reads labels on cans*): Purple. Emerald

Green. Day-glo Orange. (*To* JANE *who has slowly stopped thrashing and has risen to her knees in order to see better.*) You'll see, this is going to be great! (*He tosses paint can and brush at her.*) Start with this. Day-glo looks great on boobs. Be free!

Dashes out. Colored balloons float in. He re-enters, carrying large tin tub. Inside the tub sprawls enormous female store-window dummy.

Snap it up! Can't you get those cans open?

Exits. Re-enters carrying phonograph and movie projector. Turns them on: deafening loud rock, accompanied by a light show. Light show intensifies, becomes blinding. The last action we see is DICK *leaping through air at* JANE, *an open umbrella in his hand. After a suitable lapse of time the rock record ends, the light show goes off, the room is black.*

O boy, O boy, O boy, O boy, O boy. Did you ever dream it could be that good? I've never had it that good. Don't you feel good, Jane? I feel good. Don't you feel loose, like your limbs are floating in air? Don't you Jane? The best I ever had it. I'll have to tell you about the other times. Christ, we've got so much to talk about, Jane. You know, it's crazy, but I feel so close to you, as if for the first time I've seen you—I've seen what you're really like—I've seen your soul. And you've seen my soul, Jane. What does good or bad or ugly or sick mean when we've seen each other's souls? Listen to me talk. I never talk this way, you should know that if anybody does, but now you've got me talking a mile a minute, I can't stop. Would you believe it's me, Jane? Janie, honey, come lie in my arms for a minute. (*He lights a match.*) Jane. Where are you, Jane?

Match provides enough illumination for him to be seen crawling out from under overturned tub. He finds the lamp somewhere on the floor and turns it on. The room is a shambles, debris everywhere, the bed is broken.

Jane! (*He starts going through debris.*) Hey, Jane! (*Looks under tub.*) Where are you? (*Looks under bed, goes through blankets.*) Jane! Hey, Jane! Hey, weren't you here? Don't tell me you missed it! Jane! Jane! (*Opens door.*) Jane! (*Exits, his voice fading as he disappears down the hall.*) Jane! You should've been there! Jane!

His voice dies. Lights fade.

End